JAZLYN O'S
BIRTHDAY CELEBRATION

May all of your birthdays be HAPPY!
Renná Bruce

Written by **Renná Bruce**
Illustrations by **Robin Oakes**
Illustration colouring and page design by
Kevin Strang & **Mandy Strang**

Visit www.jazlynj.com for more information on the Jazlyn J series!

Published in Canada by
Jazlyn J and Company Inc.
www.jazlynj.com

Library and Archives Canada Cataloguing in Publication

Bruce, Renna, 1969-

Jazlyn J's birthday celebration / Renna Bruce ; illustrations by Robin Oakes ; illustration colouring and page design by Kevin Strang and Mandy Strang.

ISBN 1-894933-78-8

I. Oakes, Robin, 1973- II. Strang, Kevin, 1955- III. Strang, Mandy IV. Title.

PS8553.R818J39 2002 jC813'.6 C2002-905690-X

I would like to dedicate this book to my parents, Dave and Darlene, who made sure every birthday I had was a celebration! And to my brother, Randy, who never wanted to miss a thing during an all-girls birthday party sleepover and got his head stuck in the stairs making sure he didn't!

Renná

Dedicated to my sister Tracy and her daughter Julie.

Robin

At 7 a.m. on July 7th, Jazlyn J woke up and smiled. This is it, she thought, today is my birthday! As you read on, can you guess how old she is?

She got dressed and put on her fuzzy green slippers…
her favourite of the 7 pairs she owned!

Then she went downstairs and kissed her parents good morning. They were up already and seemed to be in a great mood. She sat down at the table and found 7 pancakes on her plate!

“Happy Birthday Jazlyn!” her Mom smiled. “I hope you enjoy your breakfast. I have a special treat for you when you’re done!”

"I can't believe it's your birthday again," her father commented. "It seems like we just celebrated your sixth birthday! And now…well, I just can't believe it!"

"It means I'm a big girl now!" Jazlyn grinned. Her front tooth was missing, because she lost it 7 days ago, and when she smiled she could feel a little draft of air. It tickled and she often stuck her tongue through the hole.

After breakfast, Jazlyn's Mom blindfolded her and took her over to the kitchen counter. It took just 7 steps.

When the blindfold came off, Jazlyn was excited to see a beautiful chocolate cake, and on it, there were 7 candles!

In the dining room, Jazlyn found 7 party hats on the table and 7 plates! Can you guess how old she is turning now?

That's right! 7! Seven is a special number for Jazlyn. There are 7 days in the week, she owns 7 pairs of green shoes, she has 7 shelves of books in her room, and her Mom says she took just 7 hours to come out of her tummy!

In the living room, Jazlyn found 7 balloons (all green, of course because that was Jazlyn's favourite colour!) and 7 goodie bags waiting to be passed out. Jazlyn couldn't wait for her friends to come over.

The door bell finally rang, and Jazlyn's Mom opened the door to find 7 kids holding 7 presents for Jazlyn! Her Mom invited them in.

“Thanks for inviting us, Mrs. J!” said one of Jazlyn’s best friends, Crystal.

"I can't wait to play pin the tail on the donkey!" said Jazlyn's other best friend, Amber. Crystal and Amber lived just a few houses down, and Jazlyn had known them for (yes, you guessed it…) 7 years.

After their lunch of 7 hot dogs, they topped it off with 7 pieces of cake and ice-cream! Then, they played 7 games!

Finally, Jazlyn opened her 7 presents, and said 7 Thank you's.
Then, it was time for everyone to go home.

Jazlyn was tired, and after dinner and a bath, she was ready for bed. It was 7 o'clock.

That night, after her teeth were brushed and her pajamas were on, Jazlyn and her parents sat on her bed, ready to share their favourite parts of the day. It was something they did every night, and it was something Jazlyn really looked forward to.

“My favourite part of today was seeing my little girl turn 7 years old!” her mother said with a warm hug.

“My favourite part was eating that delicious cake!”
her father licked his lips and smiled.

"I have SO MANY favourite parts! Today was so much fun!" Jazlyn grinned from ear to ear.

"How many parts would you like to share with us?" her mother asked Jazlyn.

Can you guess what she said?

"SEVEN!" Jazlyn giggled. And with that, she listed them all and kissed her parents good night.